Nuclear Pakistan and Nuclear India: Stable Deterrent or Proliferation Challenge?

George H. Quester

The BiblioGov Project is an effort to expand awareness of the public documents and records of the U.S. Government via print publications. In broadening the public understanding of government and its work, an enlightened democracy can grow and prosper. Ranging from historic Congressional Bills to the most recent Budget of the United States Government, the BiblioGov Project spans a wealth of government information. These works are now made available through an environmentally friendly, print-on-demand basis, using only what is necessary to meet the required demands of an interested public. We invite you to learn of the records of the U.S. Government, heightening the knowledge and debate that can lead from such publications.

Included are the following Collections:

Budget of The United States Government
Presidential Documents
United States Code
Education Reports from ERIC
GAO Reports
History of Bills
House Rules and Manual
Public and Private Laws
Code of Federal Regulations
Congressional Documents
Economic Indicators
Federal Register
Government Manuals
House Journal
Privacy act Issuances
Statutes at Large

NUCLEAR PAKISTAN AND NUCLEAR INDIA:
STABLE DETERRENT OR PROLIFERATION CHALLENGE?

George H. Quester

November 25, 1992

******

****

Comments pertaining to this publication are invited and may be forwarded to: Director, Strategic Studies Institute, U.S. Army War College, Carlisle Barracks, PA 17013-5050. Comments also may be conveyed by calling the Director or Research via commercial (717) 245-3234 or DSN 242-3234.

FOREWORD

Nuclear proliferation, a security issue which has transcended the cold war, has been, and is, particularly troublesome in South Asia. There, India and Pakistan, neighbors with unresolved disputes since they were granted independence at the end of World War II, are believed to have nuclear weapons (although the leaders of both nations deny it) and are intermittently engaged in conflict with each other.

Professor Quester has examined this unique nuclear relationship, analyzing the attitudes and behavior of both nations. He concludes with a paradox: both have "bombs in the basement," if not in their respective military inventories, and these weapons present serious dangers to the world simply because of their destructive potential, even if their leaders have the best intentions. On the other hand, Indian and Pakistani leaders appear to have low levels of concern about each others' nuclear (not conventional military) developments. It is possible to be optimistic and conclude that the relationship is actually stable and, like the U.S.-Soviet nuclear relationship of the cold war, helps prevent war on the subcontinent, or to be cynical and conclude that each regime cares more about the prestige of membership in the nuclear club than the ominous threat posed thereby against their populations.

The Strategic Studies Institute is pleased to publish this report as a contribution to understanding the challenges of international security in the post-cold war era.

GARY L. GUERTNER
Acting Director
Strategic Studies Institute

BIOGRAPHICAL SKETCH OF THE AUTHOR

GEORGE H. QUESTER is Chairman of the Department of Government and Politics at the University of Maryland, where he teaches courses on defense policy and arms control and on U.S. foreign policy. He is the author of numerous books and journal articles on international politics and international security.

NUCLEAR PAKISTAN AND NUCLEAR INDIA: STABLE DETERRENT OR PROLIFERATION CHALLENGE?

South Asia has settled into a worrisomely peculiar relationship on the spread of nuclear weapons. Government spokesmen for India and Pakistan have been saying seemingly identical things in the comparison of their countries: "We know that *we* don't have nuclear weapons; but we have to assume that *they* have them."

This emerges against a background where India, of course, detonated what was officially described as a peaceful nuclear explosive (PNE) in May of 1974--and has not detonated any such explosives since, but nonetheless has been accumulating what could be a significant amount of reprocessed plutonium. In the same years, Pakistan, under Presidents Zulkifar Ali Bhutto and Muhammed Zia ul-Haq, evaded the world's export restrictions and worked hard to develop an ability to enrich uranium; none of this was halted under Prime Minister Benacir Bhutto. Pakistan has not detonated any nuclear explosives, but such detonations are hardly needed anymore for any state to be reasonably certain that a bomb will explode, and there are also rumors that the Chinese have offered Pakistan advice on the design of a nuclear warhead.[1]

We are thus at a stage where each nation, in the absence of international inspections and safeguards to assure anyone to the contrary, may be accused of having nuclear weapons. Adversaries may be inclined to worst-case assumptions where there is ambiguity about one another's capabilities. The outside world, including many nations which are adversaries to neither India nor Pakistan, may similarly have to be inclined to be pessimistic when so much is in doubt, and hence to conclude that both nations must have nuclear weapons.

A possibility remains, of course, that Pakistan has in effect been bluffing, that it has not really managed to enrich so much uranium for bombs yet, and has merely been letting the rumors circulate to get a deterrent impact or prestige for free. It is also possible that India has used much of its plutonium (so the Indian Atomic Energy Agency has indeed claimed), so that it can not have a large inventory of nuclear weapons. As things stand, the outside world can not verify this one way or the other.

Some Paradoxical Layers of Optimism and Pessimism.

How much do the South Asian powers then live in fear of each other on the nuclear front? How troubled are they by the lack of verification and information? The answer is complicated, and beset with paradoxes.

Because of the close historical ties between Pakistan and India, and the ease with which a citizen of one country could pass for the other, it is not so unthinkable that each side's intelligence agencies may have penetrated the decision processes of the other, i.e., on a scale comparable to the networks of spies that passed between East and West Germany, far exceeding what Moscow burrowed into Washington or vice versa. The Western military attaches and ambassadors in the South Asian capitals have often come away impressed with the details each knows about the plans and intentions of the other. In one situation, we would have called this espionage, but in another it would be "verification by national technical means," for it ought to leave each side less required to go to worst-case assumptions, by having more real information.

Yet, when it comes to their interpretation of the details of what they learn about each other, both the Indians and Pakistanis also draw criticisms from foreign embassies for tending to leap to hostile and suspicious theories, typically seeing more deviousness and antagonism in their adversary than their friends in the outside world would have found reasonable. Thus, as we noted at the outset, each side tends to tell foreigners that the other side must have nuclear weapons. Only a few officials in each capital lean occasionally in the opposite direction, noting instead that newspaper accounts tend to be sensational and pessimistic, or noting that the other side might be having difficulties making maximum use of the fissionable material production capacities attributed to it.

Yet, we then rise to a third level of each side's "intelligence" about the other, where the bulk of officialdom moves again to a surprisingly optimistic note, namely that it is highly unlikely that the other side would ever dare or choose to use its nuclear warheads. Indians voice the same phrases about Pakistanis here that Pakistanis voice about Indians, asserting that it is arrogant of outside powers to fear that nuclear warheads are any more likely to be used between India and Pakistan than between France and Britain, or between the United States and China or formerly the USSR. Is this a seriously held conclusion, reflecting again some special channels by which each is privy to the thinking of the other, or some special understanding between "brother South Asians"?

When asked to indicate which of the opposing side's intentions and momentums are the most bothersome, each side's spokesmen have been much more likely to talk about F-16s and AWACS, or tanks or aircraft carriers, or about suspected assistance to Sikh or Sind separatists, than about the possible accumulation of nuclear warheads.

How can we explain a continuing tendency to assume the worst about the adversary's capabilities on the nuclear front, and the best about his intentions? There are at least three possible explanations for this bizarre agreement between what most people have been saying in Islamabad and in New Delhi. First, each side may simply be quite mistaken, not facing up to the enormity of the destruction that could be imposed by nuclear weapons on millions of helpless people, and not understanding all the many ways such weapons could come into use. Or second, it is possible that both sides are basically bluffing here, *pretending* to be unconcerned, when they are actually deeply afraid of what the other might do with such weapons, pretending because this is important to the contest of political wills that is in progress, pretending also because neither wants to give satisfaction to the superpowers and other outsiders who have seemed so paternalistic in counselling South Asia to avoid nuclear weapons.

Or third, each side could indeed be seeing something that outsiders can not really see, a special relationship between what were formally portions of British India, a relationship that is more love/hate than simply hate, a relationship of sophistication and identification that leaves each somehow reassured that nuclear proliferation would not lead to nuclear war.

There are some peculiar limits, in any event, to the ability of either side to make nuclear threats in the South Asian context. Virtually every Indian city has a sizable minority population of Muslims. It would hence be difficult for Pakistan, given its commitment to Islamic peoples and culture, to target any of such cities with the prospect of killing so many of the very people it has always claimed to represent. Moreover, the winds blow from west to east, and it will be similarly difficult for India to impose nuclear punishment on any targets in Pakistan without suffering a deadly dose of radioactive fallout as the aftermath. Most significantly, these are considerations introduced into discussions by Pakistanis and Indians themselves, rather than being brought in by outsiders.

Such factors can be interpreted again as a part of a special South Asian insurance against capricious use of nuclear weapons, perhaps against all such use. Yet, if kinships and winds (and locations of nuclear power plants, to be discussed more extensively below) make nuclear threats so much more empty for this arena, why then the simultaneous move toward such weapons? Is it all a matter of prestige?

The Pakistani Non-Proliferation Proposals.

Pakistan had put forward as many as six different proposals under President Zia that the United States and the Soviet Union, and the many other outside powers concerned with heading off nuclear proliferation, would have welcomed, including having each South Asian state sign the NPT, or otherwise accept full-scope IAEA inspections.[2] All were declined by India, on various arguments, some of which seem disingenuous and far-fetched, others of which may have more plausibility.[3]

As part of all the paradoxes and ambiguities we are sorting out here, one might also ask whether the Pakistanis would really have welcomed an Indian acceptance of such proposals, or whether they were instead bluffing about their endorsement of such non-proliferation arrangements, confident that India would reject them. (The analogy to President Reagan's origination of the "zero option" INF proposal, on the assumption that the Soviets would probably reject it, is obvious.) It might have been a fascinatingly clever ploy for the Indians suddenly to accept one or another of the Zia suggestions, and thus to see Pakistan lose support in America and elsewhere, as it had to renege on its own proposals. But (again with the INF analogy in mind), if India had accepted the Pakistani proposals, Pakistan might then have felt trapped, and both sides might then have actually been trapped.

The Minor Issue of Delivery Systems.

It has to be stressed that our attention should be directed here to nuclear warheads, and not to the delivery systems needed to carry such warheads. The distances to most of the plausible targets in the confrontation between India and Pakistan are short, and the array of conventional delivery systems that can also carry nuclear weapons is more than sufficient to put cities like Rawalpindi and Lahore and Bombay and New Delhi at risk. For some very elegant discussions of possible counterforce attacks, whereby either side would try to disarm the nuclear forces of the other, rather than to direct countervalue attacks against cities, the additions of missiles or of higher capability aircraft delivery systems might become more relevant.

But the hard fact for South Asia is the same as for the Middle East: the crowding of populations into urban areas has packaged up a great number of easily attacked targets. One would hardly want to be visiting one of the cities mentioned if a nuclear war had begun, somehow counting on any defects of delivery systems as an assurance against nuclear devastation. The current world concern about Indian tests of missile systems, or a possible Pakistani acquisition of similar systems, is thus understandable, but may be relatively misplaced.

Some Mutually Understood Advantages of Avoiding Detonations.

Assessing what each state's general population thinks about the nuclear equation is not so simple. When the Indian government proclaims that "India does not have nuclear weapons," some voters and some opposition politicians seize on this to protest that India is being left defenseless in the face of Pakistani or Chinese threats. Yet the evidence is that very many Indians are indeed quite sophisticated about all this, enough to be assuming that their country is only a screw-driver turn away from a double-digit nuclear arsenal "in the basement," and thus to be content and pleased.[4]

The Pakistani public had also, under President Zia and under Prime Minister Benacir Bhutto, been given its governments' official line that no nuclear weapons are being sought, and responded with occasional signs of protest at this--in face of the Indian threat, but with lots of knowing winks--at the prospect that there are also indeed Pakistani bombs close to assembly.

Both societies thus seem to have a desire for bombs, but each, despite the burdens of illiteracy and poverty, also displays a fair amount of sophistication on how a bomb in the basement might thus offer most of the advantages of an overt nuclear stockpile, without incurring its costs.

Interviews with officials in Islamabad demonstrate how well the Pakistani government understands the disadvantages of either detonating a device or proclaiming a weapons program, as compared with a policy of simply leaving some ambiguity in place. In effect, the Pakistanis have been emulating the Israeli pattern of the past two decades, rather than the Indian action of 1974, even though this would naturally enough be a comparison they would resent.

Demonstrating that the Indian government understands the advantages of a policy of avoiding detonations is much more obvious and easy: India has not detonated any nuclear explosions since the one in 1974, thereby setting the world's record for waiting until the second detonation. Every other entrant into the nuclear weapons club, the United States, Soviet Union, Britain, France and China, proceeded to follow the first detonation with many more.

One has indeed heard Pakistani officials enunciating a low-key endorsement of a mutual avoidance of testing, as they claim positive results for the course they have pursued in making their country *able* to explode a nuclear device. "By our policy, we are keeping the Indians from resuming testing."

One also has heard the case made, in both India and Pakistan, that India lost more, politically and otherwise, than it gained when it detonated a bomb in 1974. The enhancement of international prestige was no longer what it had been for China a decade earlier in 1964, as some of the novelty had worn off, and as the world no longer regarded mastering the physics of nuclear explosions as such a great accomplishment. The resentment of the outside world, not just of the nuclear-weapons states, but also of a very large number of Third World states and other non-weapons states, was manifest. The reductions in economic aid to India were tangible, and the particular loss of aid to India's nuclear program was a serious setback for whatever New Delhi had intended to do in nonmilitary nuclear endeavors.

Is There Any Meaning In "Weaponizing"?

If both the South Asian states are astute enough to see this reasoning, and thus to avoid an overt announcement of a nuclear weapons program, as well as avoiding any more detonations even of a "peaceful nuclear explosive," how much importance should anyone attach to what is now another much-discussed threshold distinction, the various steps that are often cited as "weaponizing"?

Many of us would be skeptical and cynical as to whether this distinction means anything at all. To repeat, the Indian PNE was a bomb for all practical purposes, with various people around New Delhi in 1974 indeed being witty in referring to it as "the peaceful bomb."

Yet the Indian government sticks by its claims that "we have no bombs"; and the outside world (amazingly to this author) has in the past decade again begun posing a question to itself on "whether India will decide to get bombs," if Pakistan or China or some other state does this or that, i.e., whether New Delhi will "weaponize" its nuclear program. Apart from just coming out with an open statement that "we have bombs," making the weapons status declared and overt, what else could possibly be involved here?

The world assumes, and the South Asian publics assume, in the absence of inspection-supplied evidence to the contrary, that India may have between 25 and 75 nuclear weapons, drawn from the reprocessed plutonium at its disposal, and that Pakistan may now have three or four such weapons, made with the uranium it has been enriching.[5] Such bombs would indeed be typically kept slightly disassembled, for elementary reasons of safety. If such bombs were thus never quite completed, but were always simply a few turns of the screw away, this might indeed help the national leaders of either India or Pakistan look an American ambassador in the eye while saying "I can assure you that we have no bombs." Perhaps they could even pass a lie-detector test because of this useful verbal quibble. But surely this can not be what any outside analyst would be defining as "weaponizing," for this would be a very slender reed indeed, as the bombs could be assembled for use in a matter of days or hours, rather than weeks or months or years.

What else could "weaponizing" then be referring to? Attention is sometimes directed to whether aircraft are being adapted to carry nuclear weapons, with allegations that F-16s have to be given special racks or hard-points for this mission. But such adaptations may hardly be required any more, for no one's first nuclear weapons are today going to be as crude and huge as the bombs dropped on Hiroshima and Nagasaki. The device detonated by the Indians in 1974, or its Pakistani equivalent, could be transported on most fighter-bombers or air transports, to devastate the cities of South Asia.

If one wished to make the "weaponizing" distinction more meaningful, the definition should perhaps instead shift to training. There is (happily) as yet no evidence that either the Indian or the Pakistani militaries are being trained in the techniques of using nuclear weapons, or even in the responses that would be required if the other side uses nuclear weapons. Diplomats in New Delhi thus draw some reassurance from an assumption that the teams that would deliver Indian nuclear weapons to targets in Pakistan (or in China or anywhere else) are not yet being assembled, and that the standard operating procedures are not being developed.

Yet this kind of restraint is more meaningful for some contingencies than for others. It is an assurance that neither South Asian power is planning to introduce nuclear weapons on a first-strike basis early in any war. One does not nuclearize a conventional war, in hopes of winning the victories that otherwise would go to the other side, without first exercising the command and control arrangements that will be required, without first carefully training one's troops in the targets to be attacked, and in the precautions to be taken against matching responses from the other side.

Yet this distinction indeed means nothing for the more basic nuclear deterrence role for which nuclear warheads are classically intended. *If* China or any other state had launched a nuclear attack on an Indian city over the past decade, what does anyone in the world expect that the Indian government would have done with the expertise it has accumulated on "peaceful nuclear explosives"? Almost certainly, it would have slapped some bombs together and sent some small group of its air force on a desperate mission of revenge. Can anyone really believe the opposite? And would not the same be true for Pakistani responses, regardless of how little "weaponizing" had been done, if India or anyone else today launched a nuclear attack against a Pakistani city? Similarly, if Pakistan were threatened with a *total* conventional defeat, with the elimination of its entire independence and raison d'etre, would not any Islamabad regime see itself in a position of "use them or lose them"? And the same, of course, in the somewhat unimaginable situation of India suffering a total conventional military defeat and being "pushed into the sea."

The Western world has at times waxed enthusiastically about various battlefield applications of nuclear weapons, applications about which we would all be wise to be skeptical. The evidence is clear that neither India nor Pakistan have weaponized in the sense of planning for, or becoming enthusiastic about, such uses of nuclear weapons. So far, all well and good.

But there are also the more basic applications of nuclear weapons that we have just listed, uses that are not so silly or ill-advised, namely deterring someone else's use of such weapons by the threat of a matching response, *and* deterring someone else's dream of a total victory in a conventional attack. For these basic purposes, much less advance training and preparation of delivery systems are needed. For these purposes, India and Pakistan have almost surely already "weaponized," by any meaningful sense of the term.

In short, nuclear weapons already exist, with the weaponizing distinction being logically meaningless, for the two most standard situations of nuclear deterrence: the prevention of a use of such weapons by an adversary and the prevention of a total conventional defeat. For these purposes, it would suffice if a very small team of air force and nuclear program officials had coordinated on the location of the bombs in the basement, with the "basement" always being within easy reach of an airfield. Our model might be the small number of U.S. Army Air Force officers in 1945 who were privy to the Manhattan Project, the few on the island of Tinian who actually knew that a B-29 was taking off with an atomic bomb on board.

Outsiders sometimes speculate about whether such a contingency-team conspiracy, with its rudimentary basic training and coordinating and planning, could be carried off in an open society like India without anyone knowing about it. Given how rumors fly, one might have expected the press to detect such preparations by now if they were occurring (one might almost have expected the press to invent such preparations, whether or not they were occurring). The absence of reports of even this very small degree of "weaponizing" might thus be viewed by some as a reassurance of some strong restraints at work in New Delhi and Islamabad.

Yet it might be all too easy to erode any such reassurance, on several lines of argument. A great deal of time has passed since India crossed the line with a detonation in 1974. From 1974 to 1992 is equivalent to the period from 1945 to 1963, a span in which the U.S. nuclear program expanded fantastically. Can one really believe that the Indians who exploded a PNE in 1974 have avoided all the relevant speculation and planning over the ensuing years, giving no thought to how many such explosive warheads they could assemble if they had to, how the design could be simplified or improved, where the components are to be kept stored, near what delivery systems, etc.? If one imputed even a modicum of patriotism to such officials and military officers, moreover, would we not regard it as their elementary duty to their country to have mulled over how India would orchestrate its nuclear retaliation for anyone else's nuclear attack?

Some Gains And Costs In Hypocrisy.

The current situation could thus be much better, and it could be worse. The statements on each side may amount to hypocritical euphemisms, but they are useful nonetheless, when they serve as substitutes for nuclear detonations (or substitutes for those more honest and explicit statements of weapons intentions which drive an adversary to move still further along).

The issue has often been raised on whether the United States should continue to go along with such obfuscation and hypocrisy, as when the President has to certify to Congress that Pakistan does not yet have a bomb. If truth and honesty are the only considerations, such certifications have become very difficult, for all the reasons noted. If moderating the arms race, and reducing the likelihood or intensity of war in South Asia are also important, however, it might well make sense to go along with the posturing here.

As a signal between the sides, the South Asian hypocrisy indeed may play one more positive role. India's claim that its projects to date have been "peaceful" and "not a weapon," matched by Pakistani statements of a similar stripe, at the very least amount to a no-first-use pledge (even if neither side was aware of this logic at the outset). If I assert that my explosives are not bombs, at the minimum this keeps me from *threatening* to use such explosives in any war. All a no-first-use *pledge* really is, of course, is the avoidance of threats of such first-use, the avoidance of the verbal posturings that make more believable an escalation from conventional war to nuclear war. (This hardly amounts to an assurance of no use at all, however. To repeat, would India not use its PNEs as bombs if someone else had used nuclear weapons first against India? Would Pakistan not use its peaceful nuclear program to get even, if anyone so attacked Pakistan?)

But the case against such euphemisms and ambiguities has also now been articulated well by a number of Israeli scholars for their own country's situation, arguing that clear thinking and public debate about national strategy are made too difficult when such veils are maintained.[6] Perhaps, as part of not "weaponizing," neither the Indians nor the Pakistanis are thus thinking through enough of what they would do with nuclear weapons if they were ever to come to use them. Perhaps not enough thought is being given to the contingencies that may arise in the future, and to what the proper responses would be. Perhaps politicians are also too free, in this kind of ambiguous situation, to do what they find expedient--to influencing election outcomes for instance--without referring to the real preferences and needs of the electorate at large.

Fears of Preemptive Counterforce Strikes.

Many of our concerns about nuclear proliferation in this region have stemmed from fears of preemption, from the possibility that one country would attempt to eliminate the nuclear capacities of the other in some daring "counterforce" attack. Ever since the first discovery of the Pakistani uranium enrichment facility at Kahuta (located bizarrely close to the Indian frontier), or certainly at least since the Israeli attack on the Iraqi reactors at Ossirak, there has been speculation about the possibilities of such an Indian attack on the Pakistani facilities.

How real have such risks been? In a way, these risks are inherent in any relationship of nuclear deterrence. Such deterrence depends on each side being able to inflict countervalue retaliation on the population centers of its adversary. But such deterrence would then lapse whenever a counterforce first-strike can be executed so expertly that it would preclude all of the countervalue second-strike.

Yet, to repeat, if the scenarios of such an Indian strike are to be taken so seriously, why was there not more concern about such a Chinese attack on the Indian facilities? China did not race to attack the Indian facilities, and the Indians did not race to expand their nuclear force in a seeming fear of such a Chinese attack. If the Indian protestations of peaceful intent since 1974 can be taken seriously, they are at least supported in that there was no urgent and rapid move to a full-fledged strategic nuclear force in the wake of India's first detonation.

The Chinese-Indian experience is encouraging, suggesting that the power of world opinion, or more realistically the presence of other nuclear powers in the world, precludes the "nth" nuclear weapons state from preemptively attacking an erstwhile "nth plus one." China was kept from ever cashing in on its nuclear monopoly viz-a-viz India by an obvious factor: it did not have a nuclear monopoly against the rest of the world, especially against the United States and the Soviet Union.

Yet the Israeli attack on Iraq amounts to evidence in a more worrisome direction, suggesting (even if we do not take Menachem Begin's explanations of that Israeli air attack entirely at face value) that we can not totally discount such preemptive counterforce moves.

As another sign that such thoughts are never totally out of mind, the reaction of the residents of Rawalpindi and Islamabad was virtually unanimous when the ammunition dump exploded early in 1988--that this must be an Indian or Israeli attack on Kahuta. As noted earlier, the high point of such fears and tensions and apprehensions may now be behind us. Yet the years since the Ossirak attack of 1981 have seen repeated rumors of Indian plans for such an attack, or of Israeli plans for such an attack, or of Israeli proposals to the Indians that there be some sort of joint attack. All of them unconfirmable, the rumors include allegations that the Israelis have been offering the Indian government intelligence data on the nature and status of the Kahuta facility, and have been urging that the Indian Air Force attack "before it is too late."

There are rumors also that some files were somehow stolen from Indian Prime Minister Indira Gandhi's office, and then later recovered, with one of the files being labelled "Kahuta attack." Given the inherent nature of staff preparations and contingency planning in any of the militaries around the world, it would be amazing if no such attack has ever been analyzed or contemplated in New Delhi, for the patriotic duty of any staff officer is to consider *all* the options. The development of contingency plans and options thus hardly proves that such an operation was being considered seriously, anymore than the hundreds of other "war plans" that get designed around the world.

Why indeed did the Pakistanis locate their facility so close to the Indian border, barely some 40 miles away, a matter of minutes or seconds of flying time for a fighter-bomber, and an easy mark for aerial reconnaissance? One hears suggestions that the intent was to keep the facility further away from the Middle East and from the prospects of Israeli (or other) air attack from this direction. One also hears speculation that the intent was to keep the facility close to the capital and hence under more reliable central government control, less exposed to the fissiparous tendencies that might infect the Sind or Baluchi or Northwest Frontier regions. This would introduce the issues of domestic command and control, a most serious problem with any nuclear proliferation into such an unstable region, a problem which we shall have to discuss more extensively and worrisomely below.

As noted, the worst may indeed be over, as the prospect of a "splendid first strike" eliminating every possible Pakistani nuclear weapon becomes more difficult with each year that the Pakistanis have been enriching uranium. Perhaps this was already indicated by Prime Minister Gandhi's sudden 1985 offer to the Pakistanis of an agreement to ban attacks on the nuclear facilities of either country. Was this the definitive signal that India had shelved any such plans and speculations, and was now seeking to relieve any unnecessary tensions and apprehensions on the Pakistani side?

The Vulnerability of Nuclear Power Plants.

Yet there was another kind of reason for India to offer such an agreement, beyond assuring Pakistan that an Indian preemptive attack was no longer being contemplated. The large reactors constructed around India for the purposes of producing electrical power may themselves be very vulnerable to a conventional air attack, amid estimates that such an air raid could indeed produce a countervalue disaster fully comparable to an outright nuclear attack; while there would be no nuclear explosion and fireball, the radioactivity released could dwarf what was expected at Chernobyl or Three Mile Island, killing large numbers of people, destroying food production, forcing mass evacuations and panics.

Some European analysts contemplating the same possibilities for the nuclear reactors installed in Eastern and Western Europe indeed minted the phrase "nuclear deterrence without nuclear weapons," arguing that the reactors in place in any particular country achieved some of the same deterrent strategic impact as an actual deployment of nuclear weapons.[7]

If any of this was real, it meant that India, in the very process of committing itself to nuclear power production, had already produced "nuclear weapons for Pakistan," offering some of the same second-strike options that we have been tracing to the Pakistani acquisition of enriched uranium; Pakistan might not even need its own atomic *bombs*, on this line of argument, since it could effectively destroy Bombay by attacking the reactor at Trombay, etc.

The 1971 war with Pakistan already saw Indian air defense resources deployed to protect Indian nuclear facilities against the inherent threat of a Pakistani air attack. There was no Pakistani feint recorded against such targets, but the mere fact of the reactors' vulnerability tied down some Indian resources regardless of Pakistani moves.

Since India has much more of a nuclear power grid than Pakistan, this creates a somewhat asymmetrical deterrence mechanism in favor of the Pakistanis. As noted, the meteorological fact that the winds normally blow from west to east would also cause residual destruction to reach India after any nuclear attack on Pakistan, or even after a conventional attack on Kahuta or other Pakistani nuclear facilities.

In any event, all of this amounted to a powerful argument for the Indian government not to attack Kahuta, for fear of the Pakistani retaliation that would be directed against Indian reactors. A policy of mutual restraint would indeed have made sense here for both the South Asian states, regardless of whether the tentative verbal 1985 agreement between Prime Minister Rajiv Gandhi and President Zia had ever been spelled out in detail and signed. The wording of such an Indo-Pakistan ban on attacks on reactors was apparently very close to a final agreement even before Zia's death, with the actual formalization being held back by India because of the many reports of Pakistani assistance to Sikh terrorists, reports which made the proclamation of such an agreement politically inopportune. The occasion of Prime Minister Benacir Bhutto's first meeting with Rajiv Gandhi, at the Islamabad SAARC summit conference of December 1988, was then used to proclaim the agreement.

While domestic support for Indian nuclear activities, peaceful or otherwise, is overwhelming, a rudimentary antinuclear movement also had been developing among intellectuals in the country, a movement opposed to nuclear electrical power on grounds of safety and ecological damage, and opposed to any deliberate or inadvertent acquisitions of nuclear weapons. Such sentiments were somewhat reinforced, of course, by the events at Chernobyl, all the more since some of the new power reactors to be installed in India were to be imported from the Soviet Union (albeit of a design very different from Chernobyl). Yet the pro-nuclear feeling among the Indian electorate is still much stronger than the antinuclear, with Indian state governments actually competing to be the next to be assigned such a power reactor. Electricity is still in short supply in South Asia, and many Indians have regarded the ecological outcries about Three Mile Island and Chernobyl as false alarms, as someone "crying wolf," against the background of the opportunity costs when poverty is prolonged by electrification being postponed.

Worries About Command and Control.

It is easy to outline the inherent drawbacks of nuclear proliferation, simply by noting the conflicting demands of assured retaliatory capability and of responsible and reliable command and control. This is a dilemma which must inherently beset Pakistan, but which also has to be a problem for India.

If Pakistan had ten atomic bombs, and if it were afraid of some Indian counterforce attack intended to destroy this stockpile, it would be wise to disperse the ten bombs, and the aircraft to carry them, to ten different locations. But Pakistan has also been beset by regional dissidence, and (even though the military is predominantly recruited from the Punjab) by threats of military coups, as one senior general might decide that another had served too long in the role of national leadership, or that civilians could not be trusted with power. Having the nuclear weapons at remote locations would thus increase the problems of command and control, in that they might fall into the hands of someone defying the authority in Islamabad. Yet if that authority were to try to avoid this by keeping all the bombs close at hand, we would be back to our first problem again.

India continues to deny that it has nuclear weapons, and somewhat downplays how much fissionable material it could have at the moment, free of international safeguards, and free of other materials so that it could be used to make bombs. Outside estimates are higher than Indian government estimates on how many bombs worth of plutonium there may be in India. In any event, the Indian authorities have plans for amassing a sizable quantity of reprocessed plutonium for use as fuel in breeder reactors. Would India keep all of this fuel in one place, tempting Pakistan or China, or anyone else, to attack with conventional or nuclear weapons in hopes of eliminating the possibility of Indian nuclear weapons by a single stroke? One hopes that the Indian government would not be so foolish as to leave everything at one location.

India, with its democratic traditions, has had less reason to fear having its domestic rivalries played out through the threats of nuclear civil war. Yet this is also a country where a Prime Minister was assassinated by her own Sikh bodyguards. If the Indian authorities decide to disperse their fissionable materials to more than one or two locations, this would only be prudential as an insurance against some Pakistani attempt at a "splendid first strike"; yet it similarly again increases the chances that some separatist or other form of terrorist activity might come to control the makings of an atomic bomb.

India maintains tight security around its nuclear facilities, which is consistent with bomb intentions, but surely is consistent also with an elementary fear of Pakistani conventional attack, and with an elementary fear of terrorism. Indeed one would not expect or want to see lower levels of security around genuinely peaceful reactors anywhere else in the world.

Similarly, if the Pakistan Air Force remains under firm command and control, but fears the power of the Indian Air Force, might it in some future war or crisis be deployed westward to bases around the Persian Gulf, as it was once before, in the war of 1965? Would the most prized possession of such an air force, its nuclear warheads, thus be deployed to Iran or Jordan or Saudi Arabia? And what then would be the implications for who controlled such weapons and determined their future use?

This leads us into all our worries about the "Islamic bomb" phenomenon,[8] worries which may be very exaggerated but which nonetheless are inescapable, simply because of the instabilities and command and control concerns we have already had to note for Pakistan.

The comments of officials in Islamabad have been fairly reassuring that no light-hearted sharing of nuclear weapons with Arab or other Islamic countries would ever be undertaken. Even if Zulkifar Ali Bhutto wrote of "an Islamic bomb" (and there are now allegations that this portion of his memoirs is an Indian fabrication), his stress might rather have been on the *Islamic* rather than on the bomb. Perhaps the mere fact that *any* Islamic country had achieved such weapons would be a source for joy among all Islamic countries, without bombs then actually having to be shared with all such countries.

For what it is worth as reassurance, officials in Pakistan are able to articulate quite fully the worries of others about bombs slipping into the hands of various Middle Eastern states, in a way that shows that such officials at least are not missing the pitfalls of any such sharing.[9] If there are Middle Eastern states (perhaps Libya or Iraq or Iran) that would like nuclear weapons, there are surely other Islamic countries that very much do *not* want such states to get bombs, and these countries have made their feelings known to the Pakistanis over the years as well.

Pakistanis also show some awareness of the costs they would suffer if nuclear proliferation were to become worldwide--if dozens and dozens of countries were to duplicate what India and Pakistan have done. At the least, there is a perception of the advantages, in terms of lower stimulation to such open-ended proliferation, of maintaining the more subtle and covert style that has applied to date.

Optimistic or Pessimistic Conclusions?

How bad, therefore, is the nuclear situation we are outlining here, if each side now rests at such a short time-lag from bombs in the basement? After all is said and done, a very strong case can yet be made that the subcontinent, and the rest of the world, would be much better off if all of such South Asian nuclear proliferation could be avoided, for there are simply too many ways in which such nuclear weapons, once they have come into existence, can still come into use, despite the plans and best intentions of each side. And, above all, there is too much destruction that such weapons can inflict.

Defending their own nuclear program, Pakistanis point at times to the pre-existing Indian program, noting that the number of bombs that New Delhi might control has to be an order of magnitude greater than what is possible, under any assumptions, in Pakistan. Yet all of such discussions of "orders of magnitude" are misleading, as any analysts of nuclear balances could explain very easily. The comparison of the numbers of bombs on the two sides, as has also been true for the confrontation between the United States and the Soviet Union, has never been as important as the ratio of one side's bombs to the other side's densely packed cities, and very small nuclear arsenals can make a decisive difference by this yardstick. The important shifts in the situation have thus been two: at some point in the 1970s, India developed the ability to devastate a number of Pakistani cities; and at some point in the 1980s, Pakistan developed a similar ability to destroy Indian cities.

To make another comparison, showing how much we already have had to worry about in South Asia, the plausible stockpile of Indian nuclear warheads for a number of years has been greater than what the U.S. nuclear weapons total was in 1946 and 1947. And, we must presume the Pakistani nuclear arsenal to be moving into the same range.

But we are still stuck with some of our paradox of the start. Most of each side's major political figures continue to express very low levels of concern about the *nuclear* developments on the other side, as if these were far less significant than another purchase of tanks or fighter planes, or another round of support for Sikh separatists.

When Americans or other outsiders thus stress their horror at how the crowded cities of South Asia might suddenly suffer the fates of Hiroshima and Nagasaki, they are described, with Pakistanis and Indians typically using the very same words, as "preaching," as "patronizing" all of South Asia by underestimating the maturity and rationality of its leaderships. One hears statements about how much all South Asians are brothers, amid reminders about how many families straddle the partition lines of 1947, and with arguments that mutual assured destruction can work just as well for South Asia as it has worked for Central Europe, preventing war rather than making it more horrible, actually perhaps preventing war *by* making it more horrible.

Some Policy Implications.

As we compare the nuclear proliferation risks in Iraq and Iran, or in the Koreas, with the parallel case in South Asia, several important differences may emerge for U.S. policy. To begin, India and Pakistan are further along in terms of getting close to nuclear weapons, indeed in terms of how many bombs they may already have. But, as noted throughout the review above, India and Pakistan are also considerably further along in how they discuss the nuances of mutual nuclear deterrence, and on how they may limit what they aspire to do with nuclear weapons. Such discussion in New Delhi and Islamabad is more than any mere mirroring or copying of the Soviet-American dialogue. For example, the Pakistani-Indian nuclear competition appears to be dominated by a regionally strategic, bipolar relationship. Despite the often-quoted fears of an "Islamic bomb," one looks in vain for Pakistani references to extending deterrence to or sharing technology with other Islamic states in the region. If extended deterrence is not a component of Pakistani strategic thinking, U.S. policy and strategy in the region might be spared worrying about Pakistan as a regional proliferator of weapons of mass destruction.

We at least need to hear out the arguments of South Asians. Have we outsiders all been missing something about the ways in which Indians and Pakistanis can understand and trust each other, on this one particular question of whether *nuclear* weapons, once developed, will be used? If we are generous in our interpretations of candor here, we might yet extract some strands of optimism from the statements of the South Asians; if they are truly even partially as unconcerned and reassured as they often pretend, we could come away more reassured ourselves about stability in the region.

If we are more skeptical, however, we may yet conclude that this is just an obtuse posturing by two regimes which each have cared more about the prestige of having attained nuclear weapons than about the threat posed thereby against their populations.

ENDNOTES

1. For a reference to such rumors, see Leslie Gelb, "Pakistan Links Peril U.S.-China Nuclear Pact," *The New York Times*, June 22, 1984.

2. See Neil Joeck, ed., *Strategic Consequences of Nuclear Proliferation in South Asia*, London: Frank Cass, 1986.

3. A broader discussion of the merits of these arguments can be found in Dieter Braun, "Pakistan," in Harald Von Muller, ed., *A European Non-Proliferation Policy*, Oxford: Clarendon Press, 1987, pp. 187-190.

4. Based on interviews in various Indian cities.

5. A comprehensive overview of the trends here can be found in Leonard S. Spector and Jacqueline Smith, *Nuclear Ambitions*, Boulder, Colorado: Westview, 1990.

6. For example, Shai Feldman, *Israeli Nuclear Deterrence*, New York: Columbia University Press, 1982.

7. On the general role of peaceful nuclear power plants in war situations, see Bennett Ramberg, *Nuclear Power Plants as Weapons for the Enemy*, Berkeley: University of California Press, 1985.

8. Steve Weissman and Herbert Krosney, *The Islamic Bomb*, New York: Times Books, 1981.

9. Interviews in Islamabad.

U.S. ARMY WAR COLLEGE

Major General William A. Stofft
Commandant

****

STRATEGIC STUDIES INSTITUTE

Acting Director
Dr. Gary L. Guertner

Acting Director of Research
Dr. Thomas L. Wilborn

Author
Dr. George H. Quester

Editor
Mrs. Marianne P. Cowling

Secretary
Ms. Rita A. Rummel

******

Composition
Daniel B. Barnett

CPSIA information can be obtained
at www.ICGtesting.com
Printed in the USA
LVOW03s1323260716
497844LV00018B/338/P